W9-BHS-571

CHEROKEE

OCT 2 - 1990

SCIENCE IN ACTION

THE LIVING WORLD

The books in the SCIENCE IN ACTION series are

Light and Sound

The Living World

The World of Numbers

Fun with Chemistry

Projects in Physics

Experiments in Physics

SCIENCE IN ACTION

The Marshall Cavendish Guide to Projects and Experiments

Compiled and revised by
Sue Lyon

THE LIVING WORLD

Projects created by
Paul Berman and Keith Wicks

Marshall Cavendish Corporation · New York · London · Toronto · Sydney

Introduction

This book will help you learn more about science and technology. It includes experiments, projects, puzzles and even some tricks. Some of the experiments and projects are very easy. Others are a little harder (they are marked ✧) and you will need help from one of your teachers or parents. You don't have to begin on page 8 — look through the book and start with something you like — but remember that good scientists
- make a record of their work
- have a clean and tidy laboratory
- most important, keep themselves safe (always read pages 40 to 42 before you begin).

PLANTS

Plants are living things that use sunlight to live
and grow. The earth contains an enormous number
of different plants, ranging from tiny mosses to the
giant Californian redwood tree. Plants are essential
to us because they make the oxygen that we must
breathe to stay alive.
In the following pages, learn how plants germinate,
how they make their own food and how they move to
follow light. And you can grow a garden in a bottle,
see how to make plants change color, and give a
pumpkin green hair!

Germination

You will need—

4 beans
4 sheets of blotting paper
4 clean, clear jars
steel wool
refrigerator

The early stages of a seed's growth into a plant are called its germination. Though seeds usually germinate in the soil, there is nothing to stop you from growing your own inside a jar so that you can see exactly what stages it goes through. You can change the conditions inside the jar to see how the seed's growth is affected by keeping it in the dark, feeding it more water, or putting it in a colder place.

Procedure

1. Although you can use almost any seed to experiment with germination, the best one to use is a **bean**.
2. Take a clean, clear **jar** and cut a piece of **blotting paper** to fit inside it. Line the jar with the blotting paper.
3. Push one or two seeds down between the blotting paper and the glass of the jar. Position each seed about 1 inch (2.5 centimeters) from the bottom of the jar.
4. Wet the blotting paper so that it is thoroughly moistened, but do not over-water and leave a pool in the bottom of the jar.
5. Place the jar in a warm room with plenty of light. Keep an eye on the blotting paper to insure it does not dry out.
6. As the seeds absorb water, they will swell up. After a day or two, the outer coat of the seed will split as a small root appears. The root will gradually grow downward. If the seed was growing in soil, this root would hold it in place firmly.

7. After another day or two, you will see a fluffy mass appearing at the base of the root. These tiny strands are the thousands of root tip hairs that help the root to absorb moisture.
8. Eventually, a shoot with small leaves will grow upward from the seed. The leaves will be creamy yellow until they have been exposed to the light for a while, then they will turn green. This is because the green pigmentation, that many plants have, comes from chlorophyll—which is only produced when the plant is exposed to light.
9. As well as water, the plant needs food. During germination, this is provided from supplies within the seed. As the plant grows, these supplies are used up and the seed shrivels. But when the plant is exposed to light and chlorophyll is produced, the plant is able to photo-

Did you know . . .

In temperate climates, like that of the U.S., most seeds germinate every spring, as the sun's rays and light increase and rain brings needed moisture. But in some desert regions, where it may not rain at all for many years, seeds can lie dormant (which means sleeping) for years in the dry soil. Then, sudden freak storms bring much rain in a few hours. Within hours the dormant seeds have germinated and the desert blossoms into a sea of flowers. After a few days the hot sun shrivels the plants, which die—leaving fresh seeds sleeping in the sand.

synthesize—it produces its own food—at which point its germination is over.

10. As a further experiment, it is worth seeing what conditions affect a seed's germination. Make up two more jars identical to your first one. Put one into a refrigerator and another into a warm, dark cupboard.

11. Make up a third jar but do not moisten the blotting paper, and leave it in sunlight. Make up a fourth jar but replace the blotting paper with moistened **steel wool**. Put a cap onto this jar and place it in a warm place with plenty of light.

12. After a few days, check the jars to see what effect the different conditions have had. The seeds in the refrigerated and dry jars will have remained the same, showing that warmth and moisture are both required for germination to occur.

13. The seed in the jar with steel wool will have grown a little, but not much. The steel wool will be rusty—the rusting uses up the oxygen in the jar. The oxygen starvation stunts the seed's growth.

14. Finally, check the jar in the cupboard. This will have grown much like the original seed, showing that light is not required for germination of bean seeds, although some seeds do need light. But the seedling will not be green—remember it will only produce chlorophyll in light. If you left the seedling in the dark, once the food supply in the seed had run out, it would simply shrivel up and die. Without light the plant cannot photosynthesize and produce food.

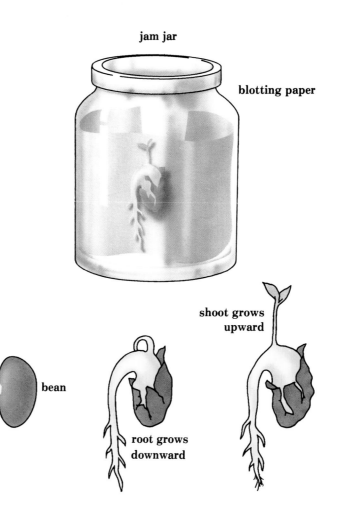

jam jar

blotting paper

shoot grows
upward

bean

root grows
downward

Phototropism

2 cardboard boxes of
    different sizes
matt black poster paint
1 block of wood or some
    books (to raise the
    cardboard box)
2 potted plants
1 sharp craft knife

Phototropism is the ability of a plant to turn toward the light. Many plants that create chlorophyll have the ability to do this, since they depend on photosynthesis (which requires light) to produce food. By turning their leaves toward the light, maximum photosynthesis can take place.

Procedure
1. Make sure you use a **green plant** for this experiment —plants that do not produce chlorophyll will not turn toward the light.
2. Place the plant in its pot in a **bright airy room** for a while. Be sure that the light in the room is not coming from any particular direction (bright sunlight through a small window, for example).
3. In the meantime, find an **old cardboard box** with a lid—an old shoe box is ideal. If you do not have a box with a lid on it, make a lid to fit any box you do have. It is very important that the box should keep out light completely.
4. Now paint the box, both inside and out, with **matt black poster paint**. This will make sure that no light can get in if the cardboard is not very thick. It also prevents light from reflecting off the inside walls of the box. If this were to happen, the phototropic effect would not be seen properly.
5. When the paint has dried thoroughly, use a **sharp craft knife** to cut a slot approximately 2 inches (5 centi-meters) long by ½ inch (1 centimeter) wide in one side of the box. If you wish, paint the cut edges black.
6. Take off the lid, and place the box on a **window ledge** with the slot facing the light. If necessary, put books, a block of wood, or a couple of bricks under the box to bring it up to window level (see illustration).
7. Place the plant in the box on the opposite side to the slot. Place the lid tightly on the box, and leave it for a few hours.
8. When you remove the lid again, you will find that the plant has turned toward the light that is streaming in through the slot in the side of the box. To confirm your findings, turn the plant away from the slot, or reposi-tion it within the box, put the lid on and wait again. When you remove the lid, the plant will have turned toward the light again.
9. Conduct a bigger experiment with a larger box and more plants. Prepare the box as before, again painting it black. If you do not want to have to move the plants around, cut a slot in each side of the box and make covers for each slot; the covers can be held in place with pieces of tape.
10. Repeat the experiment with more plants, covering or uncovering the holes as necessary. From this you can find out whether some plants react more quickly than others to changes in the direction of light. Make sure that the extra holes are well covered, or you may get false results from stray light getting into the box.

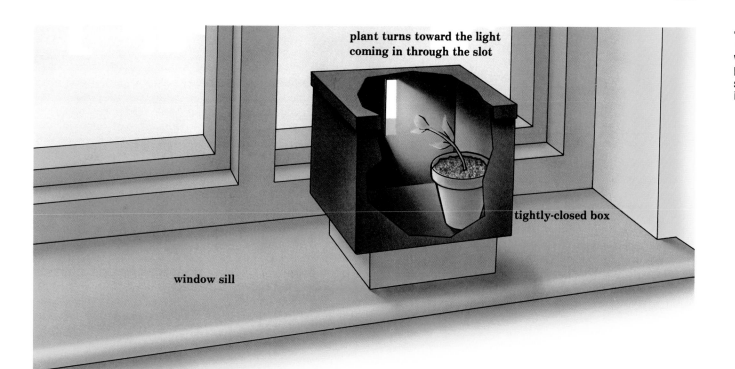

plant turns toward the light
coming in through the slot

tightly-closed box

window sill

Take care!

When using a sharp craft knife, always cut, score or slice away from your body in case the knife slips.

Bottle garden

You will need—

1 large clear glass bottle
  or carboy
2 bamboo canes, of
  medium length
1 fork
1 spoon
thin cord
gravel
charcoal pieces
compost
soil- or peat-based potting
  soil
plants such as Fittonia or
  Hedera or Maranta

Growing houseplants is a popular and decorative pastime. Every plant needs certain conditions to grow perfectly. Some types need a lot of water. Others, such as cacti, need very little. One plant will want a lot of bright sunshine, another will prefer deep, cool shade. All green plants, including their "variegated" (with patches of different color) versions, need light and moisture to grow, as well as some mineral salts. There will also be a temperature range within which the plant will grow best, and the plant, like most living things, needs air.

You get the energy you need to grow from eating food but green plants are their own food factories. The green leaves of plants contain a substance called chlorophyll which gives the leaf its green coloring. The chlorophyll reacts with the carbon dioxide from the air and uses sunlight to produce oxygen and carbon compounds such as sugars and starch. Then the oxygen is given off back into the air. This process is called photosynthesis, which means building up (synthesis) by light (photo). Plants only photosynthesize by day, but like other living organisms they respire (breathe) all the time—it is not very noticeable while the plants' food factories are working but when it is dark and the plant is not giving off oxygen, it absorbs oxygen from the air, uses it to combine with carbon compounds, and gives off carbon dioxide.

Transpiration

The process called transpiration is also going on continuously. This is the name for what happens when a plant takes in water through its roots, and feeds it up through its stem, leaves and flowers. The plant takes what it needs to keep its cells full of water and loses the rest through its leaves by evaporation. If a plant can not get enough water, particularly in hot weather, its cells lose water and become limp, so the plant droops.

This problem of water was of particular interest to the great plant collectors of the nineteenth century. The plants they found often had a journey lasting many weeks, even months, before they arrived at their destinations in the world's great Botanical Gardens. One collector, Nathaniel Ward, realized that he could seal the plants in a totally enclosed glass case with a good soil, and enough fertilizer, water and light. The plants developed their own closed-circuit system, endlessly recycling the same nutrients (food) and gases. These cases, made of sheets of glass held together by lead strips, were called Wardian cases and were very successful. The original Wardian cases were usually big structures but you can produce a similar effect for yourself at home by growing plants in a bottle garden. A bottle garden will flourish anywhere in your home as long as it gets enough light to encourage photosynthesis. Most plants that are suitable for bottle gardens will grow in ordinary household temperatures.

these special tools reach through the neck of the bottle

planting the garden

Preparing the bottle

Here are some hints on how to grow several plants in a big bottle. Not every one can get hold of a big bottle—if you cannot, try just one or two plants in a smaller bottle and remember to reduce the depth of soil. The traditional bottle for one of these gardens is an old **carboy**. Carboys have often had strong acids in them, so be very careful to use one that is clean. If you are not sure, ask for an adult's help before trying to wash it out. These jars are also very heavy.

Some garden centers and nurseries sell bottles that are specially made for bottle gardens. If you buy one of these bottles from a garden center, you can choose your plants at the same time. Ask for advice about the most suitable plants for your garden.

When you have your bottle, you will see that the neck is too narrow for either a hand or ordinary garden tools, so first you need to make some special tools. You will need two medium length, sturdy **bamboo canes** and an old medium sized **spoon** and **fork** and some **thin cord**. Bind the spoon to the end of one cane and the fork to the end of the other. Make sure they are tied on very tightly as you will put quite a strain on them when planting. If they are not tied well enough they will fall into the bottle and can be difficult to get out again.

Take care!

Wash out your carboy to insure that any chemicals it may have contained have gone. If the bottle is large and heavy, ask an adult to help you.

In the bottom of the bottle, put a layer of gravel with a few pieces of charcoal in it—the charcoal will help keep the soil in good condition. This layer should be about 1½ to 2 inches (3.5 to 5 centimeters) deep. In a large sized bottle, use a paper funnel to keep the sides clean when you add the sand and gravel. The next layer is the compost the plants will actually grow in and which will provide their trace minerals. It is best to buy soil-based or peat-based potting soil. Make a layer of about 3 to 4 inches (7.5 to 10 centimeters). Do not water at this stage or the soil will become very muddy.

Choosing plants

Now comes the exciting part—choosing which plants to put in. As a general rule you should pick plants with good foliage (leaves) of different colors and shapes. Do not use flowering plants as the flowers will be difficult to remove when they are dead. Try to get small plants from slow-growing families. What you choose will really depend on what you can get locally, but these are some plants that are suitable: Bromeliads which have long, pointed, stiff leaves (Cryptanthus has mottled leaves and is particularly useful), Fittonia—with bright green foliage with white or red veins, Hedera (ivy)—preferably one of the smaller variegated ones. Many ferns also grow well in these conditions and many need less light than most plants. Crotons have wonderfully colored foliage and are usually very slow-growing. Maranta has green leaves with purple or brown spots on the leaves.

Planting

Once you have decided which plants you want, decide on your planting plan. Generally the smaller plants should go around the outside, with the taller ones in the middle. Using the cane with the spoon, scoop a hole in the soil and take the plant out of its pot. Carefully shake off most of the soil around it. If it is a suitable shape, use the fork to maneuver it into place. If it has a lot of thick stems, use the plain ends of the cane, like chopsticks, to lower the plant into place, then firm the soil with the back of the spoon. When you have finished planting, water the plants. You can use the water to clean any soil off the leaves but do it gently. If you have put in any stones or pieces of bark, trickle the water off these.

Finally put the cork stopper in the bottle. The system you have created should thrive for at least six months without attention. If the sides mist up, open the stopper until the mist clears and then reseal it.

the finished garden
should need no attention
for six months

Photosynthesis ⊡

You will need—

2 plants suitable for a freshwater aquarium
1 glass funnel
1 clear glass bowl
1 test tube
1 sliver of wood

Green plants use energy from sunlight to form the oxygen that animals need to survive. This process is called photosynthesis. Use some water plants to make oxygen, and collect the gas in a test tube. A simple test will confirm that the gas is indeed oxygen.

Procedure

1. In a pet shop, buy a couple of **plants** suitable for a fresh-water aquarium.
2. Obtain a **glass funnel** to put over the plants, and a **test tube** to fit over the spout of the funnel.
3. Put the plants in a **clear glass bowl** or fish tank and pour in **cold water**.
4. Fill the test tube with water (figure 1) and, keeping it underwater, slide it sideways over the spout of the funnel.
5. Position the funnel and test tube over the water plants. At this stage, the test tube should still be full of water. Put the bowl or tank in a sunny place.
6. Observe how tiny bubbles of gas come off from the plants and rise up into the test tube (figure 2).
7. When the tube is full of gas, light the end of a long thin **sliver of wood** (not a *waxed* taper). Blow out the flame, lift the test tube from the funnel and quickly insert the glowing wood into the tube. The wood should burst into flame (figure 3), thus confirming that the gas is oxygen.

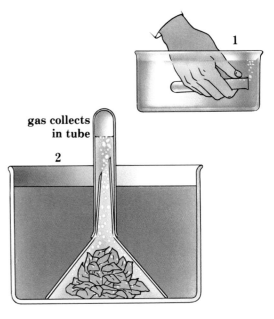

gas collects in tube

Green hair

It is very easy to surprise your family and friends by giving your Halloween **pumpkin** a fine head of green "hair." Since the hair needs time to grow, buy a pumpkin as soon as you see one in your local store.

Procedure

1. Cut off the top of the pumpkin with a **sharp knife**. Use a **large spoon** to scoop out some of the flesh (this can be used to make pumpkin pie), but be careful not to break into the soft center of the pumpkin.

2. Line the hollow you have made in the pumpkin with a layer of **damp absorbent cotton** or **blotting paper**.

3. Sow **parsley** or **grass seed** on the cotton or paper. Keep it well watered and warm until the pumpkin has a thick growth of "hair."

4. Then cut out the features of your pumpkin ready for Halloween.

1

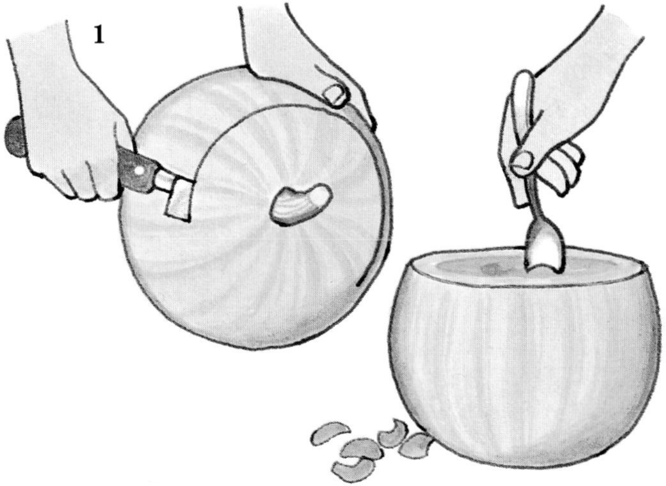

2

3

4

You will need–

1 pumpkin
1 sharp knife
1 large spoon
absorbent cotton or blotting paper
parsley or grass seed

Take care!

Be extra careful when cutting off the top of the pumpkin, since a round vegetable like this is very difficult to hold firmly. The skin of the pumpkin will be easier to cut through if you score around it with a knife before cutting.

Green flowers

You will need–

white flowers
fabric dye
protective gloves and
    clothing
1 plastic spoon
2 tablespoons of glycerine
tall container
warm water
scissors

Take care!

Whenever you use dye, protect yourself, your clothing and your working area. Mop up any spills immediately, especially if the dye touches your skin.

Have you ever seen a green flower? You can make a whole bunch of these amazing blooms very quickly, and the flowers will do most of the hard work themselves! If you want green petals, **white flowers** like carnations and chrysanthemums will produce the best results, but if you are using other colors of **dye**, you could try this technique with pale pink or yellow flowers. Before you begin, put on **protective gloves** and **clothing** and cover the working area with old newspaper. Mop up any splashes of dye immediately.

Procedure
1. Using a **plastic spoon** (the dye will color a wooden spoon), mix a box of dye powder with **two tablespoons of glycerine** in a **tall container**.
2. Add **warm water** to the mixture following the instructions on the dye box.
3. Make sure that the ends of the flower stems are not flattened; if they are, trim them cleanly with **scissors**. When the mixture is cold, stand the flowers in it. They will now "drink" the dye and they will change color in about an hour. The longer you leave the flowers in the dye, the deeper the color will be. When the color is as strong as you want it to be, transfer the flowers to a **vase or bowl** to make an unusual gift or festive display.

1

2

3

ANIMALS

The animal kingdom is vast and varied. Scientists describe beings as different as insects, fish, birds and mammals as animals since, unlike plants, they cannot make their food within their own bodies (see page 16).
In the following pages, you can find out how animals "talk" to each other and to you, and how you can make a permanent record of their tracks. You can also build your own aquarium, see how to use the shells you collect on vacation, and even make a pen from a feather.

Plaster casts

You will need—

1 small bag of plaster of
  Paris
1 round metal baking pan
1 old saucepan
paint
1 paintbrush
coins
shells

Casting provides an easy way of making copies of objects. Using plaster of Paris, you can quickly reproduce the shapes of shells to make an attractive plaque to hang on the wall. Then you can try making casts of other things, such as interesting coins and animal footprints.

Procedure
1. Buy a small bag of **plaster of Paris**. You will also need a **round metal baking pan** with the bottom removed, **modeling clay**, **shells**, an old **saucepan**, **paint** and **paintbrush**.
2. Soften the modeling clay in your hands and form it into a round flat slab. This should be slightly larger than the base of the baking pan and at least ¾ inch (19 millimeters) thick.
3. Press the bottomless baking pan into the clay. Make sure that there are no gaps between this "wall" and the clay, because otherwise your plaster cast will be irregular at the edges.
4. Press several shells into the clay and then remove them to leave impressions in the surface. Each shell can be used to make several impressions. Try to make an attractive pattern in the clay. This will act as the mold in the casting process.
5. Put cold water into an old saucepan. Then stir in some plaster, a little at a time, until you have a smooth, thick, creamy mixture. Make enough of the mixture to form a layer at least ½ inch (13 millimetres) thick over the mold.
6. Pour the plaster onto the mold and leave it to set.

Unless you are using quick-setting plaster, wait about an hour for it to harden thoroughly. (The quick-setting type should be ready for the next stage in about ten minutes.)
7. Carefully lift off the tin and peel the clay from the plaster. Copies of the shells will stand out from the surface of the plaster.
8. When the plaster is absolutely dry, you can paint it. Use a plain color for the background and try to make the shells look as realistic as possible.
9. If you are careful not to damage the clay mold when you peel it from the plaster, you can use it again and again to make several identical casts of the shell pattern.

Instead of the shells, you can use coins to make impressions in the clay. You could make several casts, each showing coins from a different country. Arrange the coins in order of value, and press both sides of each one into the clay.

Using ready-made molds
1. You can also make plaster casts using ready-made molds. Look for the footprints left in soft ground by dogs, cats, birds and other animals.
2. When you have found some clear footprints, brush away any loose surface material. Press the bottomless baking pan into the ground to enclose the marks. Then pour on the plaster mixture and remove when set.
3. See if you can identify the castings that you have made.

Did you know . . .

Plaster of Paris is made by heating gypsum (calcium sulfate dihydrate) and is called after the capital city of France because it was first prepared from gypsum found in the Montmartre district of the city. Because it dries quickly and sets hard, plaster of Paris has many applications. It is used in the pottery industry to make molds, in hospitals to set broken bones, and in architecture to make ornamental plasterwork for ceilings. And it has even been used as a material for sculpture by modern artists.

Take care!

Wipe up any splashes of plaster before they set. Once they are hard they will be difficult to remove.

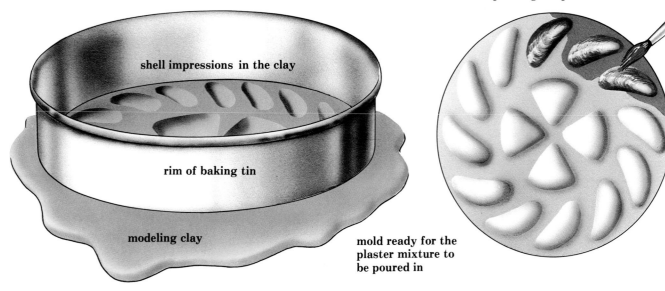

original shells

painting the plaster cast

shell impressions in the clay

rim of baking tin

modeling clay

mold ready for the plaster mixture to be poured in

Animals talking

Most people who have a pet dog or cat know when their pet is happy or hungry. A happy dog wags its tail, a contented cat purrs and hungry animals often stand beside their bowls and beg. You can tell a lot more about your pet's mood, in the same way that you can tell how another person is feeling, if you can understand the small signals that the animal or person gives. These signals, which you can learn to recognize, are called body language. Unlike humans, dogs and cats have a very small range of vocal noises that they can make, and so they use their body movements and postures a lot more for signaling their feelings.

Cats

A cat's tail is probably the most obvious signal. When a cat greets either a person or another cat, the tail is quickly brought up, given a quick flick and held vertical while the cat gives a soft vocal greeting. Sometimes the cat arches its back slightly as well, which usually causes the person to bend down and stroke the animal. Another way in which a cat signals a greeting is by moving up onto its hind legs and then down onto all fours two or three times in succession, while keeping the front legs stiff. These movements are usually used to greet human beings and seem to be specially intended to attract attention and to make us want to stroke the cat. Often, the cat will rub its head on the person's legs when he is giving this greeting.

When a cat greets another cat, it often nods its head up and down and it may also turn its head from side to side.

People sometimes play with a cat and are surprised when the cat gives them a sudden scratch or nip. If you

this cat is ready for a fight

watch carefully what the cat is doing, you should be able to tell when the cat is thinking of biting or scratching. A cat's tail being flicked from side to side means that the animal is annoyed. Often the cat will growl quietly at the same time. There is a different, more gentle, side-to-side flick of the tail that the cat gives when it is resting. This movement is just a reminder that the cat is aware of what is happening around him and that he is ready for immediate action if there is any need for it. As the cat gets sleepier, it flicks its tail less—you can usually tell how alert your cat is by seeing how often and how quickly it moves its tail. The cat's eyes also show how alert it is, because an alert animal has larger pupils that a drowsy cat.

One sure sign of annoyance that should warn you to approach your cat carefully is flattened ears. Also, rapid twitching of the ears usually means that the cat is anxious. Sometimes, ear-twitching is accompanied by lip-licking. This is not the same contented lip-licking that the cat does after a good meal, but a nervous flick of the tongue.

Cats also have a posture which they use when they are curious about something. They stare closely at the object that interests them, often stopping in the middle of some other activity, and raise one front leg slightly so that the paw hangs down.

Self-defense

The most vulnerable part of the dog or cat is its stomach. Animals will defend their stomachs by fighting with their teeth and claws. Cats often roll onto their backs and most people think that this is an invitation to play, but you should look at the cat's claws first. If his paws are limp and held well away from the stomach, he is probably looking for a game, but if his paws are held up in a defensive way with the claws showing, he may attack you if you go too near.

Many animals have a posture which they use when they are being aggressive or when they are challenging another animal. They make themselves look as big as possible by fluffing out their coats and tails. Often, the animal arches its back to try to look bigger and some animals also lean forward. An animal that is frightened will do the opposite—it will crouch down as low as possible and keep its tail well tucked in.

Did you know . . .

No animal except mankind truly talks but many use all sorts of sounds and signals to pass on simple messages. Elephants purr with their stomachs to let other elephants know that there is no danger nearby. Bats can use their squeaks to talk to one another as well as to find their prey. But the animals who come closest to language are dolphins and whales. Using a mixture of squeaks and inaudible ultrasounds, they seem to have developed a complicated code which scientists are trying to understand.

Dogs

In many ways the behavior of dogs is similar to that of cats. Both types of animal use eye-to-eye contact to try to show another animal that they are dominant (more important). A dominant dog will stare at another dog until the more submissive dog drops its eyes and shows that it has surrendered by crouching down and putting its tail between its legs. If the other dog does not surrender but returns the stare of the dominant dog, there is likely to be a fight between the two dogs.

When you meet a dog for the first time it is best to be very careful. If the dog is showing signs of fear, such as crouching down, holding its tail between its legs, leaning backward or baring its teeth, it can quickly turn into an aggressive dog that may attack. Look out for other danger signs such as the tail being raised, the hackles (the hairs on the dog's back) rising and the dog leaning forward.

A dog that wants to play also uses body language to tell you how he is feeling. A playful dog may raise his hindquarters, keep his front legs and head low, wag his tail and bounce up and down. If you play chasing and fighting games with your dog you will soon learn to tell when the dog is joining in the game and when he really is feeling aggressive.

Preparing for sleep

You may have noticed that your dog or cat sometimes turns round and round before he goes to sleep. The animal does this because he is instinctively copying what his ancestors used to do when they were living in the wild. A wild dog or cat, when he wants to settle down for the night, will make a nest for himself in the undergrowth by turning around a few times to flatten the plants and leaves underneath him. In this way, he will make a cosy hollow where he can sleep.

In addition to turning around, your pet may also make a scraping movement with his front paw. This movement, which looks as though he is trying to drag invisible objects toward himself, is another instinctive action. A wild animal would scrape leaves together to make a more comfortable bed for himself, and your pet is just making the same movements that have been passed down from one generation to the next. When you see your pet turning around or scraping, it means that he is settling down for a long sleep, rather than just taking a short nap.

A contented cat

Many cats like to lie on somebody's lap and gently dig their claws into the person's clothing. The cat then moves its front paws up and down rhythmically—some people describe this action as 'making bread'. This behavior shows that the cat is contented, because it is the same movement that he used to make as a kitten when he was enjoying a meal of his mother's milk. Kittens use their claws to hold on to their mothers' fur and they move their paws up and down to stimulate the flow of milk. This gentle movement of the cat's paws is quite different from the fierce way a cat will dig his claws in if he is frightened or angry.

Other animals, as well as birds, use body signals to display their feelings. If you study your own pet, or any other creature, you will learn a lot about this form of language and this will help you to understand animals more fully.

Take care!

Never pat or stroke a dog you do not know—it might be nervous and bite.

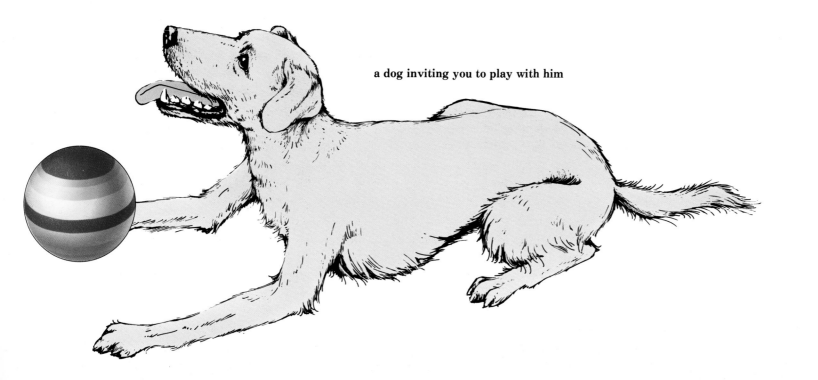

a dog inviting you to play with him

Aquarium ⊹

You will need–

fish
1 tank
water (drawn from the
  faucet)
water plants
water snails
sand
1 pail
small stones
cotton thread
1 piece of paper
fish food, such as water
  worms or water fleas

You can raise **fish** at home if you make your own aquarium. The best **tanks** are rectangular, but you can see many different types at a pet store. (Don't use round fish bowls, though; they will be too small.) As a rule, you will need 2 gallons (9 liters) of **water** for each 2-inch (5-centimeter) fish.

Goldfish, roach and stickleback are all suitable fish for an aquarium. Buy them from a pet store or collect them from a pond. Don't mix unsuitable fish such as goldfish or sticklebacks, which sometimes fight or may even kill each other. Check that your fish do not have fungus (it looks like cotton swabs), drooping fins or dull eyes. This is important since one diseased fish can infect the whole aquarium. **Water plants** and **water snails** will keep the water sweet and can be bought or collected from ponds.

The bottom of the tank should be covered with **sand** which you can buy or collect from a river or beach. Wash it well by rinsing it in a **pail** and then pouring off the water until it is absolutely clean.

Procedure
1. Put a 2-inch (5-centimeter) layer of sand on the bottom of the tank.
2. Press the plants into the sand. Anchor them until they are firmly rooted by tying a **small stone** to the base of each plant with **cotton thread**. (There will be no need to take out the stone and thread when the plants are rooted since the water will eventually rot the thread and the stones will be an attractive feature of the aquarium.)

3. Now add the water (draw it from the tap). But first, to prevent the sand from being disturbed, cut a piece of **paper** the size of the tank and put it on top of the plants and sand. Slowly fill the tank with water–leave about 2 inches (5 centimeters) space at the top–and then carefully remove the paper.
4. You are now ready to put in your fish. Feed them with **water worms**, **water fleas** and pet store **fish food**. NEVER give them bread or overfeed them–you will kill them with kindness!

put about 2 inches (5 centimeters) of sand in the bottom of the tank

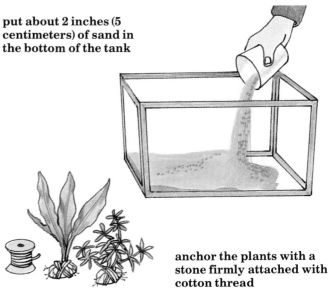

anchor the plants with a stone firmly attached with cotton thread

Take care!

Before you begin, wash out the tank to make sure that it is absolutely clean.

Even a small tank will be very heavy when it is filled with water, so it is best to put your aquarium in its permanent position before you begin work. Protect the surrounding area with lots of layers of newspaper and mop up any spills immediately.

Quill pen ⬦

Most of the writing instruments which we use today require a lot of technology in their construction. Some are very complex products, such as typewriters and word processors. But even fiber-tipped pens need the chemical technology of plastics manufacture, ballpoint pens require precision engineering, and fountain pens contain many intricately-shaped parts.

Before such technology became available, writers had to use the simpler, natural materials around them for writing. Chinese and Japanese writers favored brushes made from animal hair for drawing the complex ideograms which form the basis of their text. Early Americans followed the European tradition of using quills made from feathers. Some artists still like to use quills because they can adjust the nib size and shape to give exactly the type of line they want.

You can easily make a quill pen from a large **feather**. A 12 inch (30 centimeters) turkey feather is ideal. Wildlife parks and poultry stores are possible sources of suitable feathers. You will probably find a 12 inch (30 centimeters) feather difficult to balance in your hand when writing so trim it back as required. Most people find 7 or 8 inches (18 or 20 centimeters) best.

Dedicated quill pen users find that the barbs (fluffy parts) get in the way and therefore remove them, but you may decide that your quill pen looks more impressive with them left on. Form a nib in the end of the quill as shown in the illustration. The first diagonal cut forms the nib. The second cut forms the angle of the nib; you can experiment with a few different ones. The third cut produces a slit to improve flexibility and ink flow. The cut should be ⅜- to ½-inch (approximately 1 centimeter) long. You can adjust the width of the nib by paring away the sides.

Unlike ballpoint or fiber-tipped pens, quills will only work properly when pulled toward the writer rather than pushed away. This means, for example, that the letter "O" must be written using two separate strokes, the first starting near the top and finishing near the bottom to produce a "C" shape and the second also going from top to bottom to complete the "O".

The appearance of lettering is greatly affected by the thickness of the strokes used. This is called the weight. A typical script will have lower-case letters such as "o" seven times as high as the nib is wide. Slimmer nibs give a more delicate effect, suitable for flowing styles while broad nibs are better suited to simple letter shapes, such as Gothic alphabets. Lengths of ascenders (the tops of letters such as "b", "d" and "l") and descenders (the bottoms of "j", "g", "y" etc.), spacing between rows and spacing between letters can also be varied to produce different effects. When the adjacent parts of two letters are both vertical lines, such as "HE", a larger space is left than if one of the letters has a curved line, such as "HO" or "OH". If both letters are curved, such as "DO", an even smaller space is left. The space between words is normally about the width of a capital "O".

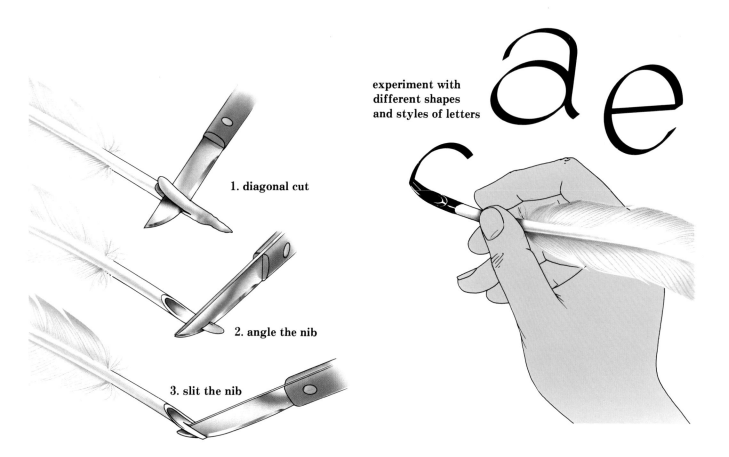

1. diagonal cut

2. angle the nib

3. slit the nib

experiment with different shapes and styles of letters

Take care!

When using a sharp knife to cut, make sure that you cut away from yourself in case the knife slips.

Be careful when dipping your quill pen into the ink not to knock over the bottle.

Using shells

small shells
1 small wooden box
1 large sheet of paper
1 pencil
glue and a brush
tweezers
clear varnish and a brush

Take care!

Do not put the glue brush down on an unprotected surface, it might stick.

Make sure that the shells are washed clean and empty before you begin.

Most people collect shells when on vacation at the beach, but once at home, it's difficult to know what to do with them. One of the most attractive ways to use **small shells** as a permanent reminder of your summer vacation is to decorate a **wooden box**. You can use lots of shells of the same kind or you can use different shells in an attractive pattern.

You should never take rare shells from the beach; instead, choose common varieties. If you are unsure about these, check in a book on shells in your school library.

Procedure
1. Put the box on a **large sheet of paper** and draw round the base with a **pencil**.
2. Arrange the shells in the shape you have drawn until you like the pattern they make. Using a **brush**, dab **glue** in the center of the box. Place a shell on the glued spot—you will find it easier to place the shell accurately if you use **tweezers.**

3. Following the pattern, glue the rest of the shells to the top of the box, working from the center outward. When the glue is completely dry, **varnish** over the whole surface of the box. This will make the shells shine and help them to stay in place.

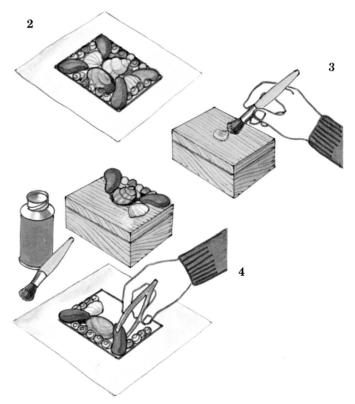

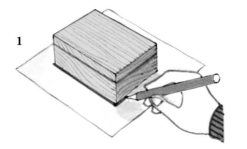

HUMAN BODY

Although scientists have created advanced computers and robots that have taken over the work of whole factories, they cannot—and perhaps never will be able to—make an android (a human-like robot) that would equal the power of the human brain or the incredible organization of the human body. (Did you know that your body contains over 50,000,000,000,000 cells?)
In the following pages, experiment with your senses of taste, smell and touch, see how to take your pulse, and learn how to take fingerprints.

Pulse rates

You will need—

1 wristwatch or clock with
  second hand
1 pencil
1 notebook

There are many ways of measuring physical fitness but most of these require the use of special equipment. One measurement that you can make easily, using just a wristwatch equipped with a second hand, is your pulse rate.

Your body automatically increases its pulse rate when you exercise so that more oxygen can be supplied to your muscles, allowing them to work harder. After you finish exercising, the increased pulse rate will continue for a time in order to flush away the chemical byproducts which are created during exercise, and which are what make your muscles ache after exertion.

To relate fitness to pulse rate, you need to measure how much the pulse rate increases during exercise and how long it takes to return to normal after the exercise ends. A minor difficulty in measuring pulse rates is that the brain can also exert an influence. Like many animals, we have a primitive reflex built into us that causes our pulse rates to increase when we are excited. For a wild animal, this reflex is very useful because excitement normally involves either fighting or running away, both of which consume much energy. Having the pulse rate increase before the muscles are used can increase the initial power available from the muscles and mean the difference between life and death. In humans, this reflex shows itself as blushing. In extreme cases, the brain may hold back the amount of blood sent to the digestive system to make more available to the arms and legs. This causes the "butterflies in the stomach" feeling which some people experience when they are nervous.

When you first try to measure your pulse rate, your brain is likely to consider the activity exciting enough

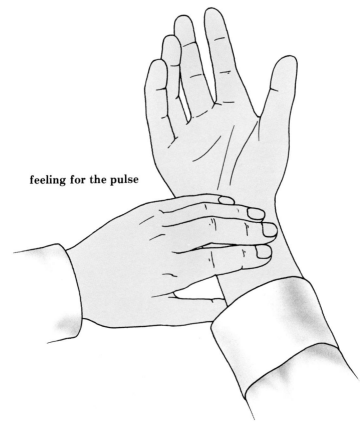

feeling for the pulse

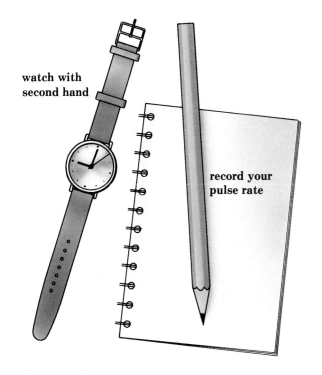

watch with
second hand

record your
pulse rate

to trigger the pulse rate-increasing reflex. Fortunately this only lasts for a short time and so can be allowed for by taking several readings and only using those when the pulse rate is steady.

Measuring your pulse rate

You can measure your own pulse rate by counting individual heart beats. You will need a **wristwatch** or **clock** with a second hand. If you are using a wristwatch, place it on a table in front of you. Lay your right forearm on the table with the palm facing upward. Relax all the muscles in that hand and arm. You should be able to see several large, dark blue veins just under the surface of your wrist. Press the index finger or middle finger of your left hand against one of these. You should now feel the rhythmic pulsing of your heart pumping blood through the vein. If you cannot feel anything, try moving your finger to a different spot. When you have found the right spot, count the number of beats in one minute as measured by the wristwatch or clock.

See how much your pulse rate increases after taking different amounts of exercise, such as walking upstairs once, running upstairs once, or running upstairs twice. Draw up a chart in a **notebook** and record all the different results. Also, check how long your pulse rate takes to return to normal after each exercise, and again record the results. Compare these results with those from other forms of exercise, such as swimming or cycling. See how your results compare with those of your friends. Now figure out the effects that different ages, weights and degrees of physical fitness seem to have on pulse rates.

Sense of touch

The human body is constantly receiving messages about the world around it. The messages are received by receptors at the end of the body's nerve fibers and passed quickly to the brain. The brain either files the information away if everything is normal, or tells the body what to do if something unusual is happening. For instance, if a heavy object falls on your toe, your brain will tell your vocal cords to say "Ouch" and your foot to move away from the object that is hurting it.

Touch and pain

One of the most important senses you have is that of touch. Without it (and the similar senses of pressure and pain) you would soon injure yourself severely in your everyday life. The disease leprosy causes the "touch" nerves to be damaged. A person with leprosy does not know that an object has fallen on his foot and damaged it unless he actually sees it happening. Even then, he has no way of sensing how bad the damage is.

There are three main types of touch receptors. One registers continuous touch sensations such as the feel of the clothes we wear, another registers intermittent touches and the third reacts to the hairs on our body being moved. These touch receptors give your brain an accurate, constantly up-dated picture of where each part of your body is and what it is doing. In fact, the brain gets so used to receiving these bits of information that people who have had a limb amputated continue to feel its presence for a long time, even feeling pain in the missing limb.

Sensitivity

Touch receptors are not spread evenly over the body but are concentrated in those areas where they are most needed to tell the brain what is going on and to protect the body from harm. The fingertips are extremely sensitive and indeed the whole of the palm of the hand is well supplied with nerve endings, unlike the back of the hand which has far fewer. You can demonstrate this with the help of a friend and a couple of well-sharpened pencils.

Place your hand flat on the table, palm down, and close your eyes. Now ask your friend to pat the points of the pencils on the back of your hand about two inches apart. Then start moving the second point closer to the first. At first, you will feel two separate points, but there will come a time when both points register as one —measure the distance between the points at this stage. Now repeat the experiment on the front of the hand and note the difference.

Your back is one of the least sensitive parts of your body. Ask a friend to touch you lightly there—you may not even notice. Even when touched harder, you may not be able to say exactly where you have been touched.

The sensitivity in the fingertips enables blind people to read. They use the Braille alphabet which consists of characters formed from sequences of raised dots on paper. Using the Braille alphabet as shown (the black dots are the raised ones), write a message with a pin and some paper. Close your eyes and see if you can read it back with your fingertips.

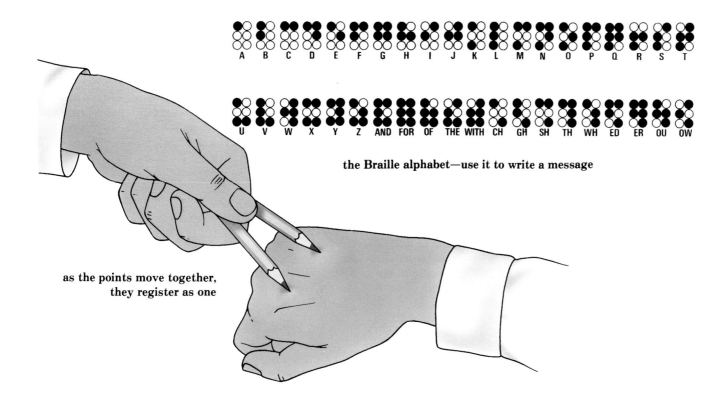

the Braille alphabet—use it to write a message

as the points move together,
they register as one

Taste and smell

You will need—

1 knife
1 plate
1 apple, cut into pieces
1 potato, cut into pieces

Have you ever noticed that when you are suffering from a cold, any food you eat does not taste quite like it should? Most people say that it is because your "taste buds" are affected. Although this is true, it is also because your taste buds depend to a large extent on *smell* to sense the flavor of your food. In general, 80 per cent of your sense of smell works through your nose—the other 20 per cent goes through your mouth. When you get a cold, your nose becomes blocked up and membranes inside become inflamed, which robs you of most of your "taste".

In addition, your eyes play a part in warning your taste buds what to expect. You would, for example, have no difficulty in telling a raw potato from an apple because it looks different. But if you take away the visual information, your brain has no way of telling what the food or drink looks like, or what color it is.

You can do an experiment with an apple and a raw potato to show exactly how much you depend on your nose and eyes for your sense of taste. It will help if you have a friend who can take notes.

Procedure

1. Cut part of a **potato** and an **apple** into slices or cubes of the same size. Place all the pieces together on a **large plate**. Make sure that it is impossible to tell which is which by feeling them, or the experiment may not work.
2. Sit down with the plate in front of you. Close your eyes and carefully mix up the slices or cubes again so that you have no idea which pieces are potato and which are apple.
3. With your eyes still closed, use one hand to pinch your nose so that you cannot smell anything.

4. Pick up one of the pieces in your free hand—your friend should note down whether it is potato or apple—and bite into it. You should find it difficult to tell what you are eating because you cannot smell the aroma of the piece in question. Do not cheat and take your fingers off your nose, or the experiment will be spoiled.
5. When you have decided what it is you are eating, tell your friend. Then carry on tasting various pieces (still keeping your eyes closed and nose blocked off) making sure your friend notes everything down.
6. Once you have finished—eating five pieces will give you a good idea—open your eyes and see what your friend has written down. You may be surprised to find out just how many times you wrongly identified what you were tasting!
7. Do the experiment using any foods that have a similar texture to each other or do it with different drinks. The results may be very different from those you expect.

Did you know . . .

Compared to most animals, human beings have a very poor sense of smell. (We make up for it by having good eyesight.) Dogs, it is thought, can smell a million times better than we can; certainly a dog can smell another's presence three miles away. Mink have an even keener sense of smell; they will travel over many miles to meet. Rodents, such as mice, rely heavily on their sense of smell to find food, for they often search during the hours of darkness. But humans probably are more influenced by smells than we consciously realize, even today.

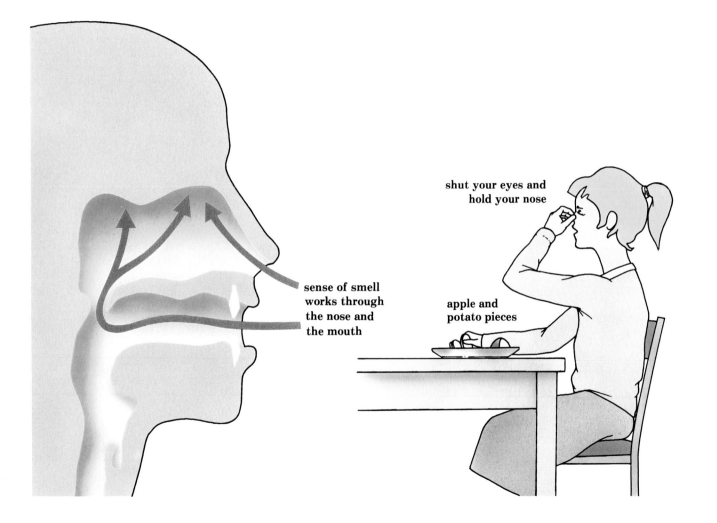

sense of smell
works through
the nose and
the mouth

shut your eyes and
hold your nose

apple and
potato pieces

Fingerprints

You will need—

1 inked pad
powder
2 brushes
1 glass or cup

Fingerprinting is widely used by police forces and other security organizations throughout the world as a means of confirming whether a suspected criminal was actually at the scene of a crime. Sometimes fingerprints are used instead of signatures to authenticate documents, particularly if the person concerned cannot write. The technique of fingerprinting works because everyone has a slightly different pattern of lines on their fingertips which remains basically unchanged throughout their lives. Our skins continually secrete sweat and natural oils over most of the surface of our bodies. When we touch something, some of these secretions are transferred to the touched object. Objects touched by fingers will therefore carry a copy of the pattern of lines from the fingertips, in other words, a fingerprint. You can demonstrate this by pressing your fingertips onto an **inked pad** and then onto a sheet of paper. You should then see a pattern like those shown in the illustration. The police use a similar method to obtain sets of reference fingerprints from suspects which can then be compared with those found at the scene of a crime.

Finding fingerprints on hard, smooth surfaces, such as doors and cups, is relatively easy. A fine, light powder is lightly brushed over the surface where it will cling more easily to areas where sweat and oil remain. This produces a visible pattern which may then be photographed. Many women have suitable **powder** and **brushes** in their make-up boxes. Alternatively, you could try powdering some pencil lead and using a fine, soft paintbrush. Start by showing up a fingerprint which you have deliberately put on the side of a cup. When you have mastered the technique, you can look for fingerprints in other places. You will probably find that fingerprints left unintentionally by other members of your family are much more difficult to identify since they will often be incomplete, overlapping, faint or smudged. On textured or dirty surfaces, the problems can be even worse. Many criminals realize that their fingerprints could give them away and they therefore either wear gloves or carefully clean their fingerprints from everything they touch.

While the basics of fingerprinting require no sophisticated equipment, many police forces are now using more advanced technology to assist them. For example, fingerprints may be recovered from difficult surfaces by making them glow under ultraviolet light.

The problems of matching fingerprints are similar to those of matching faces, that is, if you have two different pictures side by side, it is reasonably easy to tell whether they are of the same person. If, instead, you cannot see the pictures but are given a written description of them, the task becomes much more difficult. Computers have to work on the equivalent of a written description of fingerprints when they attempt to match them and so cannot normally guarantee to match fingerprints correctly. Instead, they will produce a list of the most likely possibilities which are then assessed manually by an expert. As computer technology improves, the computer is taking over an increasing amount of the routine comparison work, leaving the human experts to do the difficult parts of their jobs.

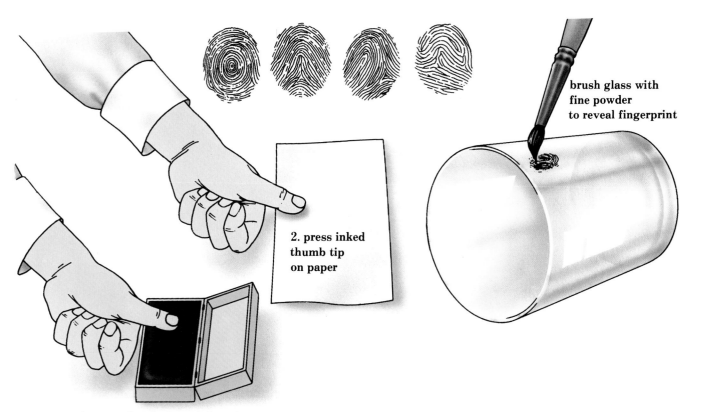

brush glass with
fine powder
to reveal fingerprint

2. press inked
thumb tip
on paper

1. press thumb tip on ink pad

Safety first!

The safe and simple projects and experiments in this book cover many fields of science and technology, and have been designed to demonstrate and explain important scientific principles in an interesting and straightforward way. Good scientists take care to protect themselves and other people, so always follow these rules for perfect safety.

*Fire Take care when using matches or candles, and keep a pail of water nearby in case of accidents.

*Main line electricity Use low power batteries as directed in this book. Do not use the main line—it can kill.

*Chemicals Use with care, label clearly, and store out of reach of young children and animals.

*Sharp edges Where possible, file edges smooth, and always protect your hands with thick gloves.

And remember . . . before you begin, always get permission from an adult, and if in doubt, ask for help!

Safety
The chemicals used in the projects can all be handled safely. Most are common household substances such as salt, baking powder, vinegar, etc.

When a project calls for an electricity supply, there is no danger of electric shock because a low-voltage battery is used.

A few projects involve the use of a flame or heat from a stove. In such cases, younger experimenters should be supervised by an adult, but the procedure is as safe as cooking.

Supervision
The projects have been graded according to the need for adult supervision. Where a project is marked with an ⊹, it means that, for complete safety, an adult should assist the young experimenter with some aspects of the project. In many cases, the adult's assistance will be limited to helping with some parts of the project, such as using a hammer and nails, and then letting the experimenter continue the project with only background supervision. Similarly, it may be necessary for an adult to handle matches or candles.

In other cases, the adult can prepare the materials which are needed for the experiment. For example, if the project includes accurate cutting out with a sharp knife, the experimenter need not handle the knife if the adult does the cutting out beforehand.

It is a good idea for an adult to be present when the project involves breakable objects like glass jars. A little guidance will minimize the risk of breakages.

Sharp edges
Wherever it is possible, the materials chosen for the projects are the safest ones that can be used. Sometimes, there is a choice of materials. For instance, the risk of sharp edges is reduced if you use plastic glass, but if you do use conventional glass, the chance of getting cut will be minimized if you are careful. First, protect your hands with gloves and use a small file or some sandpaper to remove any sharp edges from the glass. Handle the glass carefully and never put too much strain on it.

Similar precautions should be taken if the project involves cutting metal. Again, wear gloves and file off any sharp points. For extra safety, cover the cut edges with thick adhesive tape. If the project uses an empty tin can, try to find a can with a push-fit lid. This means you do not need to use a can opener, which will leave a sharp edge.

Chemicals

The chemicals used in the projects are all harmless, but they should still be treated with care. Keep each chemical in a labeled jar, and make sure that the jars are stored out of reach of inquisitive small children. Do not experiment with chemicals anywhere near food. Cover the worktable with old newspaper; it will catch any spilt chemicals and can be thrown away later. After the experiment, wash thoroughly the jars or dishes that have been used and pour the old chemicals down the sink, flushing them away with lots of water. Finally, wash your hands to remove any traces of chemicals on the skin.

Fire

You should take extra care with those projects which involve matches or candles. Organize the worktable so that there are no scraps of paper lying around and make sure that you are not wearing loose clothing, such as a tie or scarf which might accidentally catch fire. Check that you have all the materials needed for the experiment before you begin and arrange them on the worktable so that you do not need to reach over the candle. Always keep a pail of water close at hand just in case there is an accident.

Procedure

Before starting work on a project, it is important to read the instructions through to the end and to form a clear idea of what has to be done, and in what order. Materials and tools needed are listed in the margin and are spelled out in **bold type** when they are first mentioned. Make sure that everything is at hand when it is needed. Many of the projects or experiments can be carried out more smoothly if a little preparatory work, like weighing or cutting out, is done beforehand.

Science and the future

There are more and more opportunities for scientists in the modern world. Every year, new scientific discoveries help to change the world we live in. Most aspects of our life, including transport, entertainment, medicine and industry are changing rapidly because of the new inventions and discoveries that scientists are making. When you work on the projects in this book, you will learn many of the basic scientific principles which have helped important scientists to make their contribution to our world. Maybe one day, if you decide to become a scientist, you will join the great men and women of science who will create the world of the future. Who knows what you could achieve?

Words you need to know

In this book, you may find some words that you haven't seen before. These four pages explain as simply as possible what these words mean and will help you to understand exactly how to do the projects or experiments. Some words are special descriptions invented by scientists, and so are often very complicated to explain—in fact, whole books have been written about them! Of course, there isn't space in this book to include these very long explanations, but if you want to read more about any of them, ask your teacher or librarian to help you find a book.

Absorb
To take in or soak up liquids or gases

Acid
A type of sour, sharp-tasting substance that attacks metals

Aggressive
Likely to attack

Amputate
To cut off a leg or other part of the body

Aroma
Sweet or pleasant smell

Assess
To guess the size, weight, value or quality of some thing

Authenticate
To establish the truth or genuineness of some thing or person

Bark
"Skin" or covering of a tree

Body language
Way of showing feelings through body movements

Braille
Means of printing and writing used by blind people. Raised dots stand for letters of the alphabet and are "read" with the fingertips

By-products
Secondary or unexpected products of another process

Carbon compounds
The vast number of elements joined up with carbon, such as carbon dioxide, which make life possible

Cell
Most basic element of living creatures or structures

Charcoal
Black remains of partly burnt wood or bones

Chlorophyll
Substance which colors a leaf green and carries out the photosynthesis process

Compost
Mixed manure or fertilizer of organic matter such as leaves

Craft knife
Sharp knife used for projects and craft

Digestive system
The stomach and intestines that break down and absorb food

Document
Writing or piece of paper that supplies firm evidence of something

Dominant
Greatest, most important or commanding

Dormant
Asleep or resting

Evaporation
Turning from solid or liquid into vapor or gas

Fertilizer
Natural or man-made substance put onto plants to encourage their growth

Foliage
Leaves

Gas
Air or vapor

Germination
When a seed starts to grow into a young plant

Glycerine
Colorless, sweet and sticky liquid

Gravel
Small stones and sand used for road surfaces

Index finger
The first, leading finger next to the thumb

Inflame
To set fire to or light up

Limp
Not stiff, easily bent

Membrane
Pliable tissue or lining in animal or vegetable body

Mineral salts
Salts deposited in mineral layers

Nerve fibers
The bundles of nerves taking messages and feelings to the brain

Nutrient
Substance that provides nourishment

Nursery
Sheltered growing area for young plants

Organism
Living plant or animal

Peat
Decomposed vegetable matter which is used as fuel or fertilizer

Photosynthesis
The conversion of light into chemical energy

Phototropism
The tendency of plants to grow toward the light source

Pigmentation
Coloring

Plaque
Film or layer on teeth which attracts bacteria

Plaster of Paris
White powder made by heating gypsum. When mixed with water, it dries quickly and sets hard

Posture
Placing or positioning of a person or thing

Receptors
Organs that respond to light or heat

Reference
Authority to which something can be referred

Reflex
Automatic response to a stimulus

Respire
To breathe air in and out

Rhythmically
With a repeated, regular motion

Rust
Reddish coat covering iron and steel after they have been attacked by moist air

Secrete
To produce fluids, such as saliva, in the body

Seedling
Plant raised from seed, not from cutting

Sequence
Order in which things appear; set of things that belong together

Shrivel
To curl up and wither

Starch
White carbohydrate found in all plants

Stem
Main stalk of a plant

Stimulus
Thing that causes some activity or event

Synthesize
To produce artificial compounds as opposed to extracting them from plants

Taste buds
Cells in tongue which give taste sensation when combined with sense of smell

Temperature range
Degree to which temperature differs according to circumstances

Test tube
Glass flask used for testing, normally long with a rounded base

Transfer
To remove, convey or change over

Transpiration
Breathing out watery vapor through tiny pores in a plant's leaves

Trigger
To set off an event or action

Variegated versions
Types of plant or tree in differing colors or shades

Vein
Blood vessel which takes blood back to the heart

Vulnerable
Easily wounded or hurt

Index